Pocket Explorer
Ancient Egypt and the Nile

Joyce Filer

This book is dedicated to Oram, Raif and Cian (also to mum Pauline and dad Opare) for their advice, help and friendship – thank you.

Author's acknowledgements

Special thanks to Carmen Lange, Richard Barritt, Mary and Patrick Power, and Kathy Whalley. Thanks for much-appreciated help to Tania Watkins, Neal Spencer and Jeff Spencer of the Department of Ancient Egypt and Sudan, British Museum; and to Richard Parkinson and Claire Thorne, in the same department, for drawings.

For photos, thanks to Blokes At Work Productions, George Hart, Derek Welsby, Peter Clayton and the Department of Ancient Egypt and Sudan, British Museum.

Last, but definitely not least – grateful thanks to my editor Carolyn Jones for guiding me on this journey along the Nile!

© 2007 Joyce Filer
Published by British Museum Press
A division of The British Museum Company Ltd
38 Russell Square, London WC1B 3QQ

ISBN 978 0 7141 3125 2

Joyce Filer has asserted her right to be identified as the author of this work.
A catalogue record for this title is available from the British Library.
Designed by Crayon Design, Brighton
Printed by Tien Wah Press, Singapore

Illustration Acknowledgements

Main map artwork by Cally Sutherland, Crayon Design, Brighton.
Photographs are taken by the British Museum Department of Photography and Imaging,
© The Trustees of the British Museum, unless otherwise stated below.

Peter Clayton 20 bottom.
Joyce Filer pages 6 top, 7 bottom, 9 centre, 10 bottom right, 11 centre, 13 bottom, 14 bottom left and right, 15 top, 15 bottom right, 15 bottom left, 16 centre, 17 top, 17 centre, 20 top, 23 top left, 24 top, 25, 26 bottom, 30 top, 30 centre, 31 bottom right and left.
Graham Harrison pages 3, 5 top, 8 bottom, 9 bottom, 10 top, 12 bottom, 16 top, 22, 30 bottom, 31 centre.
George Hart page 9 top.
ML Design page 8 map.
Richard Parkinson page 19 plan of tomb.
Claire Thorne page 16 temple diagram, page 26 pyramid complex diagram, page 28 map.
Derek Welsby 13 centre right.

Contents

Egypt, The Gift of the Nile   4

The First Farmers   6

    A predynastic cemetery   7

The Nile Provides   10

    The desert provides   11

Ancient Nubia   12

    Pyramids at Meroe   13

UPPER EGYPT   14

Famous Temples   15

Thebes: Tombs and Mummies   17

    Mummification   18

    Inside a tomb   19

Middle Egypt   20

    New religion, new city   20

The Fayum Oasis   22

LOWER EGYPT   24

The Giza Pyramids   25

    Cat temple   27

    Delta towns   27

Egypt's Neighbours   28

After Ancient Egypt   30

Further Reading   32

Map of Ancient Egypt   after page 32

Egypt, The Gift of the Nile

Egypt was one of the greatest ancient civilizations in Africa. Today we still marvel at its pyramids, temples, mummies, and hieroglyphic writing. In the fifth century BC the famous Greek author Herodotus wrote that Egypt was 'the gift of the Nile'. He meant that the river provided rich, fertile land where people could live, farm and build. Without the Nile, Egypt would be nothing but scorching desert. All the amazing achievements of the Egyptian civilization were possible because the Nile created a land where people could live and prosper. The Nile was also the main transport system of Egypt. Boats were used to transport people, food and building materials to different parts of the country.

This beautiful painting was made for the tomb of Nebamun, an Egyptian official who lived in Thebes.

The ancient Egyptians knew how important their river was, and they gave their thanks to a special god of the river, named Hapy. In statues and paintings Hapy has the face and beard of a man but the body of a woman. This is because the Egyptians thought that Hapy was both a father and mother to their country, bringing the water that changed the desert into fertile farmland.

Statue of Hapy.

The 'gift of the Nile' – fertile land in the middle of dry desert.

The modern name 'Nile' comes from a Greek word *Neilos*, which means a valley or river valley. The ancient Egyptians called the Nile *iterw*, which in ancient Egyptian means just 'the river'.

The Nile is the longest river in the world – it travels about 7,000 km (4,350 miles) from one of its sources in central Africa to the Mediterranean Sea. Today the Nile, and the smaller rivers which run into it, actually travel through nine different countries in Africa: Uganda, Sudan, Egypt, Ethiopia, Zaire, Kenya, Tanzania, Rwanda and Burundi. On the way the river flows past mountains, swamps, rainforests, rocky outcrops, farmland and, of course, deserts. This book will take you on a journey along this famous river, visiting some special places along its banks and meeting the people who lived there thousands of years ago.

Experts think that prehistoric people first began to live in settlements in the Nile valley more than 7,000 years ago. Farming was the basis of life in ancient Egypt, so a good place to start our journey is with the first farmers.

Boats were the most important means of transport in ancient Egypt. This model boat was placed in a tomb.

5

Farmland in Egypt today.

The First Farmers

The development of farming changed the lives of the early Egyptians. The very earliest prehistoric people were hunters and gatherers who travelled around looking for food. Once people began to plant crops, they had to settle down in one place to be near their fields and to look after their animals. So the first villages and towns grew up.

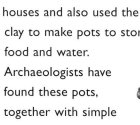

An early Egyptian pot painted with a boat. It was made in the Predynastic period – before Egypt became a single country under one king.

People learned how to make all the things they needed. They made bricks from Nile mud to build houses and also used the river clay to make pots to store food and water. Archaeologists have found these pots, together with simple jewellery, in burials.

A model showing a man ploughing with oxen.

A model showing men making mud bricks and setting them out to dry.

The Egyptians grew wheat and barley and used them to make bread and beer. They also grew fruits and vegetables such as pomegranates, dates, onions and lettuces.

A painting of farmers winnowing (separating the good wheat from the chaff).

Another valuable plant was flax, which provided linen for clothing, bed sheets and mummy wrappings. The farmers also kept animals such as cattle, sheep and goats. These animals provided milk, meat, hides of leather and wool for clothing.

Egyptian linen.

Like other early peoples, the Egyptians learned how to co-operate with one another. Farmers helped other farmers as they realised that they could not do all the work alone. In a successful farming year farmers had enough food to feed their families and they stored extra food to last through the year.

Sometimes extra food was traded, or sold, to other villages. Eventually, this meant that the Egyptians had to develop a writing system so they could record all their business and trade.

A model of a granary where crops were stored. A woman is working – the man above sits and watches!

These geese are being counted by the man on the left, who writes down how many there are.

A predynastic cemetery

One of the earliest towns we know about in ancient Egypt was Hierakonpolis. Hierakonpolis stood on the west bank of the Nile in southern Egypt. When the people of Hierakonpolis died they were buried in the hot sand, which removed moisture from the bodies and preserved them. Archaeologists have found many of these sand-dried bodies. The bodies lie curled up in shallow graves with pads of linen on them, which suggests that in about 3400 BC the people of ancient Hierakonpolis were already thinking about how to make wrapped mummies.

A burial from Hierakonpolis.

How exactly did the Nile create fertile farmland in the middle of a huge, sandy desert? The Nile starts off as two separate rivers – called the White Nile and the Blue Nile. The White Nile starts from Lake Victoria, between Uganda, Kenya and Tanzania. It flows steadily all year long.

The Blue Nile starts from Lake Tana high up in the Ethiopian Highlands and as it flows north through Ethiopia several smaller, or tributary, rivers join up with it. The Blue Nile flows weakly for most of the year, but every winter heavy rains fall in the highlands and this extra water flows into the Blue Nile. So, by the springtime, the Blue Nile is very swollen, forcing the water to flow more quickly and carry rich fertile soil along with it. The rushing water also carries lots of small plants which make the water a blue-green colour, giving the river its name. At Khartoum in Sudan the Blue Nile meets up with the White Nile and the united river flows into Egypt.

The sources of the Nile.

In ancient times, each year between July and September, the River Nile flowing through Egypt used to swell up and burst its banks. The water flooded onto the land on either side of the river. This yearly flooding is called the *inundation*.

Even today, it's possible to stand with one foot in the fertile farmland and one foot in the dry desert.

The fast-flowing waters of the inundation carried along rich, black mud which was left behind on the land, creating fertile fields in which crops could grow. The colour of the mud gave Egypt its ancient name *kemet*, which means the 'Black Land'. Following a successful inundation, the farmers planted seeds in the mud and waited for their crops to grow.

The water in the river rose to different levels in different parts of the country. The flood level was very important to the farmers in Egypt, so priests measured the water levels and recorded it on the walls of special 'Nilometers'. Too much water meant that the crops drowned and people's mud-brick houses were destroyed. Not enough water meant that the crops dried out and died. In bad years there were famines and many people died of starvation.

The Nilometer at Aswan – it looks like a flight of stairs.

Mud brick is still sometimes used for building in Egypt today.

Sometimes the Egyptians dug channels to control the floodwater and create fertile fields. They had a special way of moving water from one place to another. They raised water in a *shaduf* – this is a bucket made of leather at one end of a long pole with a weight at the other end. The pole rests on a crossbar so that the bucket and weight can be lifted up and down. In later times, the Egyptians used water-wheels pulled by oxen or donkeys.

A *shaduf* standing at the edge of the water.

The Nile Provides

A carving of men in a papyrus boat, herding cattle across the river. Note the crocodile lurking below!

In ancient times the banks of the Nile were crowded with wildlife and plants. Ferocious animals, such as crocodiles and hippos, lurked in the water. They were very dangerous to fishermen and farmers, though wealthy Egyptians sometimes liked to hunt them.

The river provided people with fish to eat, such as the Nile perch and the puffer-fish. Only wealthy Egyptians could afford to eat meat, such as beef or lamb, so fish was an important – and healthy – food for ordinary people.

Another very important thing that the river gave to the Egyptians was papyrus. Thick clumps of papyrus reeds, with large fluffy heads, grew beside the water. Papyrus stems could be taller than a grown man, sometimes as much as 3 m (10 ft) in height. People cooked and ate the pith, or inner parts, of these stems. They also burned the papyrus roots as fuel for cooking. The Egyptians wove the reeds into baskets and mats for their homes. They also made papyrus sandals, similar in style to modern flip-flops. Bundles of long stems of papyrus were tied together to make boats known as skiffs. Tomb paintings show fishermen spearing fish from these skiffs.

A model of a servant girl carrying a basket.

Papyrus reeds.

Sometimes a tomb owner is shown standing in a papyrus skiff as he tries to hunt birds flying over the river.

The most important item made from papyrus was writing paper. Strips of papyrus stems were laid side by side, one layer on top of another, and beaten to release a starch-like glue. Sheets of papyrus were pasted end to end to form a long roll. The Egyptians used these rolls of papyrus to record stories, poems and

A tomb painting showing Nebamun hunting in the marshes.

business letters. Today we know a great deal about the Egyptians and their lives because experts can read the papyri that they left behind.

This papyrus shows scenes from the afterlife. On the right the owner of the papyrus, Ani, is worshipping a god. On the left, we see idealised farming activities, where everything is fertile and successful.

The desert provides

Either side of the river were the desert lands. The Egyptians called the desert *deshret*, meaning the 'Red Land'. The desert protected the Egyptians from their enemies, because it was very hard for invading armies to cross the hot, waterless sands.

Some Egyptians bravely travelled into the Eastern deserts to hunt or to mine for precious stones, minerals and metals. In Sinai they mined for copper and for gemstones, such as turquoise, to use in jewellery.

The writing on this scarab (beetle) amulet tells how King Amenhotep III hunted lions in the desert.

The Egyptians also buried their dead in the desert. In early times, the hot, dry sand helped to preserve dead bodies and gave the ancient Egyptians the idea of making mummies.

The body of an Egyptian man, preserved by the desert sands at Gebelein.

Ancient Nubia

Nubia was the ancient name for the land to the south of Egypt, modern Sudan. The Nile flows through Nubia before reaching Egypt. Nubia was an important culture in the ancient world and, like the Egyptians, its people depended on the Nile.

Ancient Egypt had a lot of contact with Nubia: sometimes for trade, sometimes in war. The Egyptians got most of their gold from mines in Nubia so they were anxious to control the area. Some Egyptian kings built strong fortresses – like the one at Buhen – to protect the trade routes into Nubia and control the Nubian people. It did not always work. In the 7th and 8th centuries BC, the Nubians conquered Egypt, and Nubian kings ruled Egypt as the Twenty-fifth Dynasty.

An Egyptian painting showing Nubians bringing tribute of gold, ebony, leopard skins and live baboons to the Egyptian king.

Egyptian kings also built temples and monuments in Nubia to show off their fame and power. At Abu Simbel, Ramesses II built two magnificent temples, one for himself and one for his beautiful wife Queen Nefertari.

However, Nubia was not just an outpost of Egypt. We know about different groups of Nubian people who lived along the Nile creating their own important cultures. An early group lived near Faras about 3,000 BC. They made very attractive pottery which they put in the graves of their dead. Another civilization

A carving of Ramesses II in his war chariot, from inside his temple at Abu Simbel.

NUBIA

Aswan
1st cataract
PHILAE

ABU SIMBEL

BUHEN
2nd cataract
FORTS PROTECTING TRADE ROUTES INTO NUBIA

3rd cataract

Kerma
4th cataract

River Nile

GEBEL BARKAL

5th cataract

MEROE

KHARTOUM
6th cataract

White Nile
Blue Nile

(sometimes called the first kingdom of Kush) was based at Kerma between about 2,400 BC and 1,500 BC. Their palaces, temples and tombs have been studied. The objects in their burials showed they made good tools, pottery, jewellery and leather garments.

This beautifully-made pot comes from Kerma and was made between around 1750 and 1550 BC.

Pyramids at Meroe

Pyramids in the cemetery at Meroe.

From about 300 BC, Nubian kings lived at Meroe. Here there was plenty of water from the Nile and sometimes there was rainfall. The soil was fertile so cereals such as barley and also vegetables were easy to grow. The people of Meroe reared herds of cattle. Meroe also had a famous royal cemetery. The Nubians did not mummify their dead but some kings did build pyramid tombs like the Egyptians, and worshipped Egyptian gods. The most famous Nubian pyramids are at Meroe.

Part of a carved wall from the pyramid chapel of the Kushite Queen Shanakdakhete at Meroe. She is sitting on a throne with a prince and the Egyptian goddess Isis standing behind her.

Something very interesting happens to the Nile in Nubia. There are six *cataracts* between Aswan and Khartoum. Cataracts are stretches of the river where large rocks partly block the river and stop boats from sailing. Records from the Old Kingdom period tell us that a trader named Harkhuf had to travel into Nubia by donkey caravan, because his boats could not get past the second cataract.

Boulders block the river below Aswan.

UPPER EGYPT

The ancient Egyptians thought of their country as two different areas: Upper Egypt and Lower Egypt. They believed that long ago the two parts had been joined together by a powerful king, and this is why the pharaoh's titles always included hieroglyphs that read 'he of the sedge plant and the bee', meaning 'King of Upper and Lower Egypt'.

The vulture goddess Nekhbet wears the white crown of Upper Egypt. The cobra goddess Wadjyt wears the red crown of Lower Egypt. Together these 'Two Ladies' stood for the united land of Egypt and they protected the king.

From Nubia, the Nile flows into Upper Egypt (the southern part of the country). Here the climate is hotter and drier than in Lower Egypt, and this is one reason why so many things have been preserved from ancient times. Upper Egypt is sometimes also called the Nile Valley. It stretches about 700 km (435 miles) from Aswan up to Cairo in the north.

At Aswan there are huge outcrops of rock in and around the river and the desert is sometimes very close to the water. There are important quarries at Aswan where the ancient Egyptians obtained granite stone to make statues and obelisks. The stone was cut out in large blocks and then carried to different parts of Egypt by boat. As the Nile flows north within Upper Egypt, the landscape changes. The river becomes wider and there are strips of cultivated, or farming, land on both sides of the river.

Outcrops of rock at Aswan.

The desert sloping down to the River Nile.

Famous temples

The Egyptians worshipped many gods and they built temples all over the country. Some of the most famous temples were built along the Nile in Upper Egypt. One of these is called Kom Ombo. It is dedicated to two different gods, Horus the Elder and Sobek. Most of the gods of Egypt were associated with wild animals that expressed something about their character. Horus was associated with the all-seeing falcon and Sobek with the powerful

Kom Ombo temple.

crocodile. At Kom Ombo priests placed crocodile mummies and statues in a little storehouse in honour of the god Sobek.

A little further north stands the even more famous Temple of Horus at Edfu. This beautiful building is the best-preserved temple in Egypt. The walls are decorated with carvings telling us about religious life in ancient Egypt. The god Horus has the falcon as his special creature so two large, beautifully carved falcon statues guard the entrance to the temple.

Crocodile statue dedicated to Sobek.

A falcon of Horus at Edfu temple.

The pylon (huge gateway) of Edfu temple.

15

Further up the Nile is the most important and famous place in Upper Egypt – Thebes. Today it is called Luxor. The kings of Egypt built many important monuments in this area. One of the most impressive monuments is Karnak which is really a huge complex, or group, of temples. Karnak is dedicated to the chief god of Egypt, Amun, and to other gods.

Part of the enormous temple complex at Karnak.

The Egyptians believed that the gods would always protect Egypt so long as they were worshipped and given offerings in their temples. On festival days, priests took the god's statue and carried it in a procession around Thebes. Over several centuries different kings added new buildings and huge decorated gateways, called pylons, to Karnak. The temples were powerful and wealthy and many priests worked there. Like most temples, Karnak also had a sacred lake. The water was used for cleansing and purification, and for special rituals.

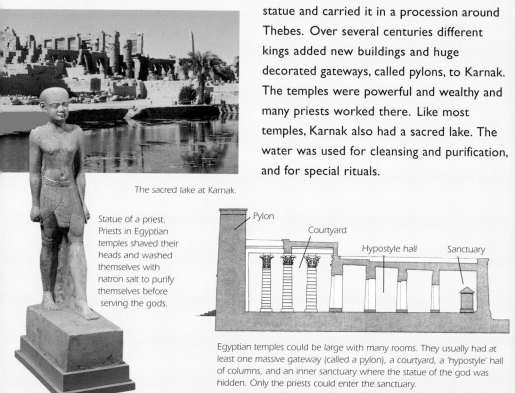

The sacred lake at Karnak.

Statue of a priest. Priests in Egyptian temples shaved their heads and washed themselves with natron salt to purify themselves before serving the gods.

Pylon

Courtyard

Hypostyle hall

Sanctuary

Egyptian temples could be large with many rooms. They usually had at least one massive gateway (called a pylon), a courtyard, a 'hypostyle' hall of columns, and an inner sanctuary where the statue of the god was hidden. Only the priests could enter the sanctuary.

Thebes: tombs and mummies

During the New Kingdom period (1550–1067 BC) Thebes was Egypt's most important town and many kings ruled the country from here, including Tutankhamun. Tutankhamun and many other New Kingdom pharaohs were buried in tombs carved into the rock of the Valley of the Kings near Thebes.

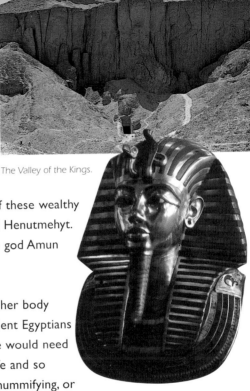

The wealthy noble people of the time also wanted to be buried in special tombs. One of these wealthy people was a lady called Henutmehyt. She was a singer for the god Amun in his temple at Karnak.

The Valley of the Kings.

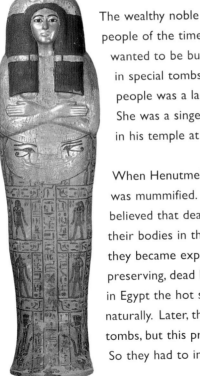

When Henutmehyt died her body was mummified. The ancient Egyptians believed that dead people would need their bodies in the afterlife and so they became experts at mummifying, or preserving, dead bodies. In early times in Egypt the hot sands of Egypt dried out and preserved bodies naturally. Later, the Egyptians began to put their dead in coffins and tombs, but this prevented the sand from preserving the bodies. So they had to invent a different way to mummify bodies.

King Tutankhamun.

The outer gold coffin of the lady Henutmehyt.

Mummification

Embalmers took out the brain and internal organs (except the heart). They covered the body with natron salt to dry it out, then wrapped the body in linen.

Once the mummy was ready for its funeral, it was loaded on to a special funerary boat and taken across the Nile to the western side. The Egyptians believed this journey across the river copied the journey made by the sun across the sky each day – so the person would be reborn in the afterlife, just as the sun rises again.

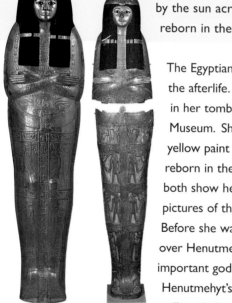

The Egyptians wanted to be buried with lovely things to use in the afterlife. The lady Henutmehyt had many beautiful objects in her tomb. Some of these objects are now in the British Museum. She had two wooden coffins covered with gold and yellow paint – this sun-like colour tells us that she has been reborn in the afterlife. The coffins fit inside each other and both show her beautiful face, her enormous black wig and pictures of the gods who will look after her in the afterlife. Before she was put in the first coffin a special cover was put over Henutmehyt's mummy – this cover shows her worshipping important gods such as Anubis. Unfortunately, only part of Henutmehyt's mummy was still inside her coffin when it came to the British Museum.

Henutmehyt's inner coffin and mummy-cover.

Henutmehyt had a special chest (or box) with four canopic jars inside to hold her mummified lungs, liver, stomach and intestines. Each jar has the head of a god as a stopper.

Her canopic jars.

She has another box containing mummified food for her journey to the afterlife – rather like a packed lunch!

A loaf of bread from a tomb.

Henutmehyt's box of *shabtis*.

A mummy needed help to find the afterlife, so a roll of papyrus was placed in Henutmehyt's tomb showing her which way to go – rather like a road map! In the afterlife she would need servants to work for her, so forty brightly painted *shabti* (or servant) figures were placed in her tomb. The Egyptians believed these figures would spring into life when Henutmehyt called them.

Inside a tomb

In Thebes tombs were usually cut into the rock of the cliffs. The burial chamber for the mummy, and store rooms for burial goods, were usually underground. A shaft led up to the tomb chapel, where relatives could leave offerings. New Kingdom tomb chapels were often beautifully decorated with paintings. Some of the finest examples of Theban tomb paintings are now in the British Museum in London. These paintings are from the tomb of a man named Nebamun (you can see others on pages 4 and 11). The paintings show us scenes of farming, hunting and fishing in the marshlands and banquets (or parties) which people enjoyed in this life and the afterlife.

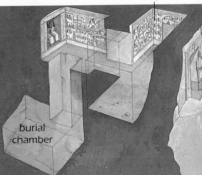
tomb-chapel

burial chamber

Plan of the tomb of Nebamun.

Party guests and a serving girl, painted on the wall of Nebamun's tomb chapel.

Middle Egypt

North of Thebes, the Nile continues through the central, or middle, part of Egypt. This is a less famous area, but some of the important places here include a new city and a fertile area right in the middle of the dry desert.

New religion, new city

One of the most interesting places in middle Egypt is a city which was used for only twenty years. The city was called Akhetaten (its modern name is Tell el-Amarna) and its ruler was one of the most unusual kings in Egyptian history.

This king's name was Amenhotep IV and he became king of Egypt in 1352 BC. His wife was the beautiful Nefertiti. Amenhotep and Nefertiti had six daughters and King Tutankhamun married one of these girls. Unlike the other kings of Egypt,

Statue of Akhenaten. He is always shown in art with an unusual body shape and a long face – unlike all other Egyptian kings.

All that remains of the palace at Akhetaten.

Amenhotep IV did not worship the god Amun (and all the other gods and goddesses). He chose to follow a new religion with only one god, the sun-disc, called the Aten. He changed his name to Akhenaten in honour of this god. He also moved the royal court from Thebes to a new capital city, Akhetaten, further up the river. The city of Akhetaten was specially

built in the desert where nobody had lived before. The new city had temples for the sun god Aten, buildings for government workers and palaces for the royal family. Akhenaten and his family were very fond of the natural world so their artists decorated the buildings with paintings of the birds, animals and plants seen along the banks of the River Nile. The non-royal people lived in houses away from the city centre and near the river. Here they grew foodstuffs and raised cattle and pigs.

This broken relief shows Akhenaten worshipping the Aten. The sun's rays pour down on him, each one ending in a hand.

After Akhenaten's death, the people of Egypt returned to their old religion and the new city was abandoned.

A piece of painted pavement from Akhetaten, with a design of birds and plants.

This lovely glass bottle, in the shape of a fish, was found at Akhetaten.

The Fayum Oasis

Much further up the river, as it flows northwards, there is a very interesting area called the Fayum. On the map you can see it south-west of modern Cairo.

The Fayum is an oasis. An oasis is a special area in the desert where there is a water-supply, so plants can grow and people and animals can live. There are several oases in Egypt's Western Desert, such as Siwa, Bahariya and Farafra.

A spring at Siwa oasis. This green area sits in the middle of hundreds of miles of empty desert.

The Fayum oasis gets water from the Nile by a small river called the Bahr Yusef. The Fayum is a very fertile region and farmers grew – and still grow – lots of fruit, vegetables and cereals. In ancient times, people also hunted and fished for extra food. We know that people started living there in the Stone Age, before 6000 BC, and it is still a very rich and successful farming area today.

A waterwheel helps irrigate the fields in the Fayum

Several Egyptian kings of the Middle Kingdom period (2055–1650 BC) chose to build pyramids in the Fayum. Some of these pyramids were made of mud brick. Experts think that King Amenemhet III built one of these pyramids and a temple in honour of the crocodile god Sobek.

At the Kom Ombo temple (in Upper Egypt) crocodiles were mummified in honour of Sobek.

The remains of the pyramid of Amenemhet III at Hawara.

Crocodile.

But in the Fayum, the priests kept live crocodiles in lakes. When Greek authors visited the area in the fifth century BC they wrote that these sacred crocodiles wore gold jewellery (they don't say how it was put on) and had servants to look after them. We are told that tourists fed the animals cakes and meat. In Greek times one of the towns was even called Crocodilopolis! The Fayum was developed further by the Greeks and Romans when they governed Egypt after 332 BC. Farming was improved so that even more food could be grown and the extra food was traded. Many retired soldiers went to live in the Fayum and records tell us that they were given plots of land to farm.

A suit of armour made of crocodile skin. The armour was made for a Roman soldier living in Egypt, after Egypt was conquered by the Romans.

The Fayum is particularly well-known for the type of mummies that were made there in the later periods of Egyptian history. Earlier Egyptian mummies wore masks of wood or gold, like that of Tutankhamun, but many of the Fayum mummies have a

realistic painted portrait instead. We think the portraits were painted when the person was alive then, when they died and were mummified, the portrait was put in place. This new way of making mummies was introduced after the Romans conquered Egypt in 31 BC. You can see that the hairstyles, clothing and jewellery in the portraits are in a Roman, not Egyptian, style.

The mummy of a man called Artemidorus.

We don't know the name of the woman who had this lovely mummy portrait.

LOWER EGYPT

Farmland near Balamun in the Delta.

The northern part of Egypt is known as Lower Egypt. It stretches from north of modern Cairo up to the Delta area and the coast. Lower Egypt covers a much smaller area than Upper Egypt.

The geography and the climate of the area are also very different. Lower Egypt is a flat area without the rocks and deserts found in Upper Egypt. The area is wet and marshy, which means it is an ideal environment for wildlife – many varieties of birds, fish and other creatures live there. Evidence from ancient Egyptian tomb paintings tells us that Lower Egypt was a popular area for hunting and fishing. The moist environment meant it was an ideal place in which to grow crops such as papyrus and flax plants to make linen. It was also more suitable for pastures where cattle, sheep and horses could graze.

North of Cairo, the River Nile splits into dozens of tributaries (smaller rivers) each following a different course to the Mediterranean Sea. This area is called the Delta. The land is much less dry than the rest of Egypt, but the rivers are full of salt from the Mediterranean Sea and this makes the soil very salty. The evidence we have tells us that many people lived here in ancient times and that temples and towns were built here as in the rest of Egypt. However, the salty and wet soil, and the intensive modern farming and settlement here means that anything buried in the ground – such as buildings and bodies – is much less well-preserved in the Delta than in the dry desert sands of Upper Egypt.

The Nile delta.

The Giza Pyramids

The most famous buildings in the world are in Lower Egypt – the pyramids of Giza. There are at least eighty pyramids in Egypt, but the Giza pyramids are the largest and by far the best-known. They were built in the Old Kingdom by three kings from the same family – Khufu, Khafre and Menkaure.

The pyramids of Giza.

The River Nile had an essential role to play in the building of the pyramids. The large blocks of limestone used to make the pyramids were mined nearby. This limestone was not the best quality stone, but that didn't matter because it was hidden inside the structure. The outside of the pyramids was covered with slabs of much better quality white limestone. This beautiful white stone was mined in the Tura quarries over on the east bank of the Nile. The slabs were dragged to the river, loaded onto boats and then ferried across the river to the west bank.

Part of the limestone covering is still visible on Khafre's pyramid.

The quarries at Tura are still producing limestone today.

In ancient times the pyramids were much nearer to the Nile than they are nowadays – over time the course of the river has changed. After the king died his body was mummified. Then the mummy was taken across the river on a wooden mortuary boat built specially for this purpose. The boat stopped at the Valley temple beside the Nile. Here prayers were said for the dead king.

Then the mummy was dragged on a sledge up a causeway (road) to a second temple close to the pyramid, called a mortuary temple. Here, after a special ceremony, the Egyptians believed the king was given the power to walk and talk again. After this the mummy was placed in the pyramid with precious jewellery, clothing and food for the afterlife.

Mortuary temple

The pyramid complex.

Causeway

Valley temple

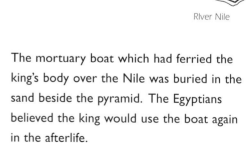

River Nile

The mortuary boat which had ferried the king's body over the Nile was buried in the sand beside the pyramid. The Egyptians believed the king would use the boat again in the afterlife.

The boat of Khufu. Archaeologists have discovered that several funerary boats are buried near the pyramids at Giza.

Cat temple

Many of the Egyptian gods had a particular city or site devoted to their worship. Bubastis (modern name Zagazig) in the Delta was the main centre for the worship of the goddess Bastet who took the form of a cat or a lioness.
A granite temple to the goddess stood in the town and thousands of cat statues were dedicated to the

Head of a bronze cat, from Bubastis.

This bronze figurine of a cat is one of the most famous objects in the British Museum.

A mummified cat.

goddess. Sacred cats were bred near the temple and when they died they were mummified and buried in underground galleries. Cats were popular pets in ancient Egypt as well as being sacred to Bastet.

Delta towns

After Alexander the Great conquered Egypt he founded the city named after him – Alexandria – in 332 BC. Stories tell us that Alexander had a dream telling him to visit the Pharos Island on the western branch of the Nile. When he arrived there he saw a huge flock of birds darkening the sky and he thought the gods were telling him to build his new city there, right near the northern coast of Egypt. Much of the ancient city of Alexandria has fallen into the sea but archaeologists are busy rescuing the palaces, temples and statues.

A coin showing the head of Alexander wearing ram's horns. The ram is the sacred animal of the Egyptian god Amun. Alexander travelled to Amun's temple in the remote oasis of Siwa, and afterwards announced that he was the son of the god.

The town of Rosetta (modern name Rashid) in the western Delta is famous for two reasons. First, this is where the famous and important Rosetta Stone was found. The Stone helped scholars to decipher Egyptian hieroglyphs. This happened because the same message on the Rosetta Stone was carved in two types of Egyptian writing, hieroglyphs and Demotic, and also in Greek. A French scholar called Jean-François Champollion was finally able to work out how to read the hieroglyphs in 1822. Secondly, the town of Rosetta is famous because this is where one main part of the Nile flows into the Mediterranean Sea, finally ending its long, long journey.

The Rosetta Stone.

Egypt's Neighbours

Ancient Egypt was a very rich and powerful country but it did not exist alone. At different times Nubians, Libyans, Assyrians, Persians, Greeks and Romans had contact with Egypt in peace and in war. They brought with them a rich mixture of languages, ideas and cultures. We have seen how the River Nile and the desert shaped Egyptian civilization, but the Egyptians also became wealthy and powerful by trading with, or by conquering, other countries.

Map of Egypt and its neighbours

Gradually, Egypt built up an empire. During the New Kingdom period (1550–1067 BC) the Egyptian empire stretched from Nubia in the south right up towards modern Syria and Turkey. Egyptian kings always showed themselves as powerful, triumphant and victorious over other countries (even if they weren't). Egyptian kings sometimes married foreign princesses to seal peace treaties, but Egyptian princesses were never sent abroad to marry foreigners.

Assyrians attacking an Egyptian town. A carving from an Assyrian palace.

Syrians bringing tribute to Egypt.

The Egyptians traded for goods that they could not obtain at home: from Nubia, they traded for gold, ivory, the skins of wild cats, live exotic animals and heavy wood for building works. From the Lebanon came logs from large cedar trees – the Egyptians used these for making large boats such as Khufu's boat, found buried at Giza. The Egyptians also bought wine from the Greek island of Crete, lapis lazuli from Afghanistan and incense from the mysterious Land of Punt, which experts think was probably Somalia. In later periods of Egyptian history Egypt bought and sold goods with Greece and Rome.

A Libyan prisoner shown on a tile from an Egyptian palace.

Egyptian scarab pendant made of blue lapis lazuli and other stones.

A carving of a man from the Persian palace at Persepolis.

After Ancient Egypt

Today, the River Nile is as important as it was in ancient times. People still use the river as a source of water for drinking and washing. They still go fishing, travel by boat, and make bricks and pots from Nile mud. However, the river has changed greatly. The inundation no longer floods the land each year. This is because two dams were built at Aswan to hold back the flood water. In the 1960s and 1970s the Aswan High Dam created an enormous man-made lake, named Lake Nasser after the Egyptian president. The water from this lake now irrigates farmland and provides electricity in power stations.

Modern felucca boats on the Nile.

The two temples at Abu Simbel, raised above Lake Nasser.

Lake Nasser covers a huge area which was once part of Nubia. The people who lived there were given new homes, and many ancient buildings were moved to prevent them disappearing under the water. Many countries in the world worked together to rescue two temples built by King Ramesses II at Abu Simbel. These enormous structures were moved, piece by piece, up the side of a mountain to raise them above the water. The beautiful temples on the island of Philae were also moved to a different island. In 2008 a huge new dam at the fourth cataract in Sudan will be finished, and this will also cause great changes.

The temple of Philae, rebuilt above the floodwater.

The environment has changed in other ways. Papyrus no longer grows wild along the banks of the Nile in Egypt. Today, Egyptian farmers grow crops, such as cotton and

otatoes, which were not known to the ancient
gyptians. The crocodiles and hippos we see in
gyptian paintings have moved away from Egypt
ecause there is no longer enough natural food
or them. They now live much further south in
udan and other places. Recently, however,
rocodiles have started to go back to the Aswan
rea – much to the surprise of some tourists, who
ometimes pass by them in small boats!

A Coptic wall painting showing Christian
martyrs. It was painted in the sixth century AD.

gyptian society has changed too. From 30 BC,
ollowing the death of Cleopatra, the Romans
uled Egypt for several centuries. Gradually, a new
eligion – Christianity – started to become more
opular. Towards the end of the 4th century AD
ll the temples of Egyptian gods and goddesses
were closed and Christianity became the official
eligion of the country. Christianity in Egypt is
nown as Coptic Christianity.

The Abu el Abbas el-Mursi mosque in Alexandria,
lit up during the month of Ramadan.

n 640 AD a general of the Caliph of Baghdad arrived in Egypt with his Arabian army
ringing with them the Islamic religion. Today Egypt is a Muslim country.
A new capital – modern Cairo – was founded in AD 969 at the very site where Upper
gypt meets Lower Egypt, near the banks of the River Nile.

The modern city of Cairo.

Many modern Egyptians make
their living from tourism.
Many visitors to Egypt enjoy
rides on camels like this one.
Suprisingly, there were no
camels in ancient Egypt before
the Roman conquest in 31 BC.

Further Reading

The British Museum Illustrated Atlas of Ancient Egypt
Delia Pemberton, 2005

The British Museum Pocket Timeline Ancient Egypt
Helen Strudwick, 2005

Draw Like an Egyptian
Claire Thorne, 2007

Pyramids and People in Ancient Egypt
Joyce Filer, 2005

The Tomb of Nebamun: Explore an Ancient Egyptian Tomb
Meredith Hooper (forthcoming 2008)

For older readers:

Cultural Atlas of Ancient Egypt
John Baines and Jaromir Malek, revised edition 2000

Encyclopedia of Ancient Egypt
General editor Helen Strudwick, 2006

Life of the Ancient Egyptians
Eugen Strouhal, 1997

You can also find lots of information and activities on these British Museum websites:

www.ancientegypt.co.uk
www.thebritishmuseum.ac.uk